Lessons on Wealth

TAYLOR J KOVAR

Lessons on Wealth
Taylor J Kovar

Interior design:
Davor Dramikanin

To my high school sweetheart,
best friend, mother of my children, and
amazing wife, Megan.
Thank you for always
believing in me.

TABLE OF CONTENTS

INTRODUCTION

True wealth is not about money. It is about freedom. Freedom from worry, stress, and anxiety about money, finances, your job, and your life. Wealth is the ability to choose your own path, instead of being forced into a role defined by others. It is the state of being able to respond to your life's true purpose without being captive to the demands of debt.

As a Christian, I believe that true wealth also entails freedom in Christ. Freedom from worry, stress, and anxiety about life, eternity, your shortcomings, and your value. It is the ability to respond to your life's true calling from God without being held captive to the demands of financial obligations.

For Christians and non-Christians alike, though, there is an epidemic of slavery, not freedom. Slavery to debt. Slavery to worry and fear about money. Slavery to "the system." A system that ensnares people early in life and never lets them escape. So many people are bound by financial obligations from which they see no hope of being freed. Although America is the richest nation on Earth, it has done a poor job of teaching its citizens how to be financially wealthy. Instead, most people live their entire lives under the weight of actual poverty or the fear of it.

I wish there was enough time for these lessons to cover all aspects of true wealth, but that would take an eternity. For now, we are going to focus on the financial side of wealth. We are going to learn how to get wealth, grow wealth, and guard wealth using principles from the Bible and other sources of financial wisdom.

These lessons are primarily adapted from principles taught in the Bible and the book, "The Richest Man in Babylon" by George S. Clason. I highly encourage each of you to read the books of Proverbs and Ecclesiastes in the Bible and "The Richest Man in Babylon". The value of the information found there cannot be overstated.

In these lessons, we will learn the three Guidelines of Wealth: Get, Grow and Guard.

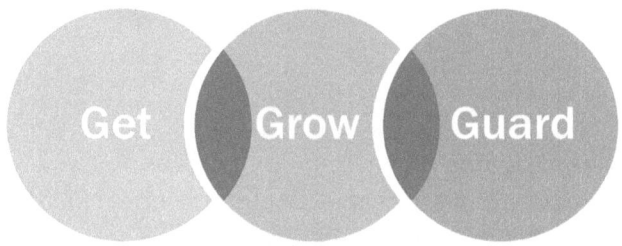

LESSON 1: HOW TO GET WEALTH

INVEST 10% OF EVERYTHING YOU EARN

Becoming wealthy does not happen overnight. It takes diligence, hard work, and discipline. Most people will never be wealthy because they choose instant gratification over long-term success. In order to get wealth, you must first invest in yourself. That means putting off some good things in order to get great things later in life.

Rule #1 is easy to learn, but very hard to live by.

> *Rule #1: 10% of what you earn belongs to you.*
> *Save it, invest it, and then make it work for you.*

You must live off of 90% (at most) of what you earn. Personally, I believe people would do better living off 80% (10% goes to the Lord and 10% to you), but that is another topic entirely! For now, suffice it to say that unless you start saving part of the money you earn, you will never have money to put to work for you. 10% is the perfect amount. Anyone, and I mean anyone, can live off of 90% of their earnings. Most times, they can live off of 90% without really even missing the other 10%. Other times, it will be a struggle to make ends meet, but it can be done. The rewards will be well worth the sacrifice.

This 10% is not a "rainy day fund" or "emergency fund". It is not a savings account that will be used to buy a large luxury item. It is a collection of wealth. It is an army of coins that will serve you. The more soldiers you enlist, the more expansive your wealth will be. This 10% is only to be used as an investment. Guard it carefully! (More on that in Lesson #3)

As you save this 10%, you will put it to work to earn you even more money. Don't be fooled by the people you see buying expensive cars, houses, and vacations. It is easy to look wealthy. It is hard to be wealthy. You can choose to work for money or have money work for you. Most people choose the former and spend their life working to pay bills and meet debt obligations. Others, the wealthy others, spend the first part of their life putting money to work for them so that later their investments pay for the new cars, the new houses, and the expensive vacations. More importantly, those investments free them financially so that they can live their lives helping others. It is nearly impossible to help others when all your effort is spent trying to pay your own bills.

Determine today to pay yourself 10% of your income. Force yourself to live off of 90% and put the other 10% to work for your future.

SCRIPTURES OF ENCOURAGEMENT

1 Chronicles 29:12

Riches and honor come from you, and you rule over all. In your hand are power and might; and it is in your hand to make great and to give strength to all.

Proverbs 6:6-8

Go to the ant, sluggard; consider her ways and be wise; who having no guide, overseer, or ruler, provides her food in the summer and gathers her food in the harvest.

1 Corinthians 16:2

On the first day of every week each one of you is to put aside and save, as he may prosper, so that no collections be made when I come.

Luke 16:10

He who is faithful in a very little thing is faithful also in much; and he who is unrighteous in a very little thing is unrighteous also in much.

2 Corinthians 9:10

Now He who supplies seed to the sower and bread for food will supply and multiply your seed for sowing and increase the harvest of your righteousness;

Proverbs 24:27

Prepare your work outside and make it ready for yourself in the field; afterwards, then, build your house.

Proverbs 13:16

A wise man thinks ahead; a fool doesn't, and even brags about it!

Proverbs 21:5

The plans of the diligent lead surely to advantage, but everyone who is hasty comes surely to poverty.

INCREASE YOUR EARNING POWER

10% of nothing is nothing. 10% of a little is a little. We now know that in order to get wealth, you must pay yourself 10% of your earnings. But if your earnings are small, it will take a long time to accumulate enough to invest. To get wealth more quickly (and to get nothing but great side effects), you know that you need to increase your earning power. Since most employers pay based upon the skill level and the value of the employee to the company, to increase your earning power, increase your value.

> *Rule #2: Make yourself more valuable. Your earning power is a reflection of your financial value to others.*

Your financial value can be calculated fairly easily. If you work for an hourly wage, your financial value is the dollar amount you earn in an hour. You are effectively exchanging one hour of your life for that dollar amount. What is your life worth? It is worth a lot more than money, but since you have to work, you might as well get paid for it! But how can you get paid more for that same hour of work? How can you earn more?

Increasing your earnings can happen three ways: 1) increase the number of hours you work, 2) increase the amount you are paid for each hour, or 3) get paid even when you aren't working. Since option #3 requires you to have resources working for you and right now you don't have any, we will have to save that option for Lesson 2. For now, let's focus on options #1 and #2.

#1. Increase the number of hours you work. The problem with this option is readily apparent. Even if you never showered, ate, or slept, you could still only work 168 hours per week. Realistically, you can only work eighty hours or less per week and maintain your sanity. Less than that if you also want to maintain your health. Increasing the number of hours you work is beneficial only as a first step to start building your wealth. It should never be the long-term solution.

#2. Increase the amount you are paid for each hour you work. Although there are limits on the amount of money you can make per hour for the work you do, it is relatively easy to increase your rate of pay by adding more value to your job. Your earning power is a reflection of your financial value to others, primarily your employer. Most employers set pay rates based upon the value of the job being performed and the number of candidates who can perform the job. A job that can be performed by any one of a billion people will have a low wage. A job that brings little value to a company will also pay a low wage. Obviously, and fortunately, the opposite is also true. A job that few people can do, or a job that brings a lot of value to a company, will normally pay a much higher wage. You can increase your earning power by increasing your value.

One of the best ways to increase your financial value is to invest in yourself. The more you know, the more skills you have, the more value you bring to a company. Many people naturally think of college as the only way to accomplish the "know more" aspect of that rule, but college is only one way to invest in yourself. The public library has thousands of print and audio books that detail topics such as business management, leadership, computer skills, writing, communication skills, sales, and countless others. The internet offers a world of knowledge, for free, to anyone willing to take the time to look. Most managers would be thrilled to put in extra hours to teach and train eager learners. All it takes is ambition, motivation, and action. By investing in yourself, you increase your earning power and in turn increase the speed at which you can get wealth.

SCRIPTURES OF ENCOURAGEMENT

Proverbs 10:4

> He who has a slack hand becomes poor, but the hand of the diligent makes rich.

Proverbs 24:3-4

> Through wisdom a house is built, and by understanding it is established; and by knowledge the rooms shall be filled with all precious and pleasant riches.

Proverbs 10:4

Poor is he who works with a negligent hand, but the hand of
the diligent makes rich.

Proverbs 14:23

In all labor there is profit, but mere talk leads only to poverty.

IGNORE THE CRITICS

One of the biggest obstacles I have seen to accumulating wealth is a
fear of criticism. Most people want to be wealthy, but very few people
want other people to be wealthy. Ironically, even though most people
think they want to be rich, very few people act like they want to rich.
Few want to be wealthy badly enough to ignore the critics that tell them
they can't be wealthy or shouldn't be wealthy. Your friends and even your
family may not understand your new lifestyle. Many (if not most) will tell
you that living off 90% of your earnings is foolish when you could use
that extra 10% to buy a [car, house, new clothes, a better lifestyle for your
kids, etc.]. By investing in your future, you are unintentionally showing
others that they are not investing in theirs. This can have serious relationship implications that many people are not able to deal with effectively.

> *Rule #3: Just because you are criticized, it doesn't
> mean you are wrong. Ignore the critics who want
> you to stay poor.*

Fear of failure, loss of relationships, and change often cause people
to do nothing at all. Don't be fooled, it is easier to simply dream of
being wealthy. It is hard to make changes that put you at odds with people you love and care about. But, like I tell my kids, if someone doesn't
want what's best for you, they don't really care about you. You are the one
responsible for your choices and your life. Ignore the critics and make
your life better. You were made by God and God doesn't make junk!

SCRIPTURES OF ENCOURAGEMENT

Matthew 6:24

No one can serve two masters; for either he will hate the one and love the other, or else he will be loyal to the one and despise the other. You cannot serve God and mammon.

Proverbs 25:28

He who has no rule over his own spirit is like a broken down city without a wall.

Luke 12:32

Fear not, little flock, for it is your Father's good pleasure to give you the kingdom.

LESSON 2: HOW TO GROW WEALTH

HAVE MONEY WORK FOR YOU

It has been said that one of the biggest differences between the wealthy and the poor is that the wealthy earn interest and the poor pay interest. Using my own not-so-strict definition, interest is the price of money. Money can only do one thing well: make more money. Interest is the process of money making more money. If you do not have a plan for your money to make more money, your money will find someone who does have a plan for it.

Most poor people do not have goals for their money, at least not tangible, written, or well-defined goals. As a result, their money follows the path of least resistance. It goes to pay bills, buy a new car, or buy any other "thing." By spending their money, their money finds a home with someone who will use it to make more money. That is why regard less of the society, culture, or economic structure of a country, there will always be poor people and wealthy people. Wealthy people know how to make money, and more importantly, how to use money to make more money.

Now that you have saved 10% of your wages, it is time to put that money to work making more money. Each dollar you have saved is now like a soldier in an army, working to bring more money to you. The more soldiers you have, the mightier your army. To increase the size of your army, you need to start recruiting more soldiers. To do this, you do two things: 1) keep saving 10% of your wages and 2) make each dollar earn more money for you. We have already covered #1 in the first lesson. Now, let's look at how money can be used to make more money.

Rule #4: Invest in assets.

The simplest definition of an asset is "something that makes money." Many people think of their house or car as an asset, but unless it earns money, it is not. Your house can be an asset, if it is appreciating in value and you plan on living in a smaller house someday. If you plan to live in your same house forever, your house is not an asset. It is a liability, unless it is making money for you.

Here are some simple ways to use your money to buy assets:

1. Invest in gold and silver when the price is low and sell when the price is high. Gold and silver will always be worth something (they have been the standard of wealth since man's creation).

2. Loan your money to someone who will pay it back with interest. See lesson #3 first, but helping other people with your money can be a valuable way for you to also grow your own money.

3. Invest in a small business. This is one of my favorite options, because:

a. It is safer than stocks because you actually get some hands-on ownership in the business

b. It is safer than stocks because you actually get to know what is happening in the business

c. It offers a higher return on investment than stocks, when you invest wisely

4. Invest in real estate. This is also one of my favorite options, because:

a. Most real estate gives you preferred tax treatment

b. Rental property gives you cash flow (from rent) plus appreciation

c. You can leverage other people's money (ie. – get a loan

from the bank to pay for the rental property)

5. Invest in stocks, bonds, and other liquid assets

SCRIPTURES OF ENCOURAGEMENT

2 Kings 4:7

Then she came and told the man of God. And he said, "Go, sell the oil and pay your debt, and you and your sons can live on the rest."

Galatians 6:7

Do not be deceived, God is not mocked; for whatever a man sows, this he will also reap.

HAVE KNOWLEDGE WORK FOR YOU

You have heard that knowledge is power. Knowledge is also money. If you had the choice between choosing ten million dollars and having a book of wisdom that told you how to make ten million dollars, you would be best served by choosing the book. Money is easily lost due to sickness, poor investments, fraud, or a thousand other calamities. If you know how to make money, however, you don't have to worry about losing your wealth. Teach a man to fish...

> *Rule #5: The more you know, the more your money grows.*

Take all the time you can to increase your knowledge. Meet people, read books, listen to experts, observe the world around you, invest in yourself. If you do that, opportunities to grow your wealth will appear to you in all kinds of strange places.

Here are a few examples of how your knowledge can help you grow your money:

1. You study real estate prices, trends, and properties in your area. When you see a property on the market below cost, you can buy it with very little down and make money when you sell.

2. You meet someone who is moving out of town and has to sell their property quickly. You can now help that person by buying the property while also helping yourself by buying property below cost.

3. You meet an investor who is looking to pool money with you to start a business.

4. You study a small business and are able to make a loan or small investment in exchange for equity or interest.

5. You track the price of any commodity (gold, silver, copper, etc.) so that when the price is low, you buy.

There are literally millions of opportunities out there. The difference between the wealthy and the poor is that the wealthy have the knowledge to see and take advantage of those opportunities.

SCRIPTURES OF ENCOURAGEMENT

Proverbs 14:15

The naive believes everything, but the sensible man considers his steps.

Proverbs 15:22

Without consultation, plans are frustrated, but with many counselors they succeed.

HAVE EVERYTHING WORK FOR YOU

Money and knowledge are two powerful resources, but if you want to be really wealthy, you will need to leverage every resource in your life to increase your army.

> ### Rule #6: Use every resource to its full potential.

Here are some resources to consider using:

1. People: wealth is only created when people use their energy to create something valuable. You don't have to do all the work to increase your wealth. Help other people create value and it will create value for you.

   a. Have your children follow the Lessons on Wealth so that they create value in your family

   b. Pay people to do work that frees you to do higher paying work

   c. Pay people to produce a product that you can sell

   d. Pool your resources with other people to create a business (ex. – you provide money, they provide the work, you split the profits)

2. Time: your time is one of your most valuable resources. Don't waste it. Most people give away hours a day of their wealth by watching TV or just goofing off. Leverage every minute of your life.

3. Other people's money: Loans and investments from friends, investors or the bank can allow you to buy real estate, a small business, or other assets that will pay for the loan plus give you a profit. If done wisely, using other people's money can quickly help grow your own money supply.

SCRIPTURES OF ENCOURAGEMENT

Matthew 25:14-30

For it is just like a man about to go on a journey, who called his own slaves and entrusted his possessions to them. "To one he gave five talents, to another, two, and to another, one, each according to his own ability; and he went on his journey. Immediately the one who had received the five talents went and traded with them, and gained five more talents. In the same manner the one who had received the two talents gained two more. But he who received the one talent went away, and dug a hole in the ground and hid his master's money. "Now after a long time the master of those slaves came and settled accounts with them. The one who had received the five talents came up and brought five more talents, saying, 'Master, you entrusted five talents to me. See, I have gained five more talents.' His master said to him, 'Well done, good and faithful slave you were faithful with a few things, I will put you in charge of many things; enter into the joy of your master.' Also the one who had received the two talents came up and said, 'Master, you entrusted two talents to me. See, I have gained two more talents.' His master said to him, 'Well done, good and faithful slave. You were faithful with a few things, I will put you in charge of many things; enter into the joy of your master.' And the one also who had received the one talent came up and said, 'Master, I knew you to be a hard man, reaping where you did not sow and gathering where you scattered no seed. 'And I was afraid, and went away and hid your talent in the ground. See, you have what is yours.' But his master answered and said to him, 'You wicked, lazy slave, you knew that I reap where I did not sow and gather where I scattered no seed. 'Then you ought to have put my money in the bank, and on my arrival I would have received my money back with interest. 'Therefore take away the talent from him, and give it to the one who has the ten talents.' For to everyone who has, more shall be given, and he will have an abundance; but from the one who does not have, even what he does have shall be taken away. Throw out the worthless slave into the outer darkness; in that place there will be weeping and gnashing of teeth.

LESSON 3: HOW TO GUARD WEALTH

After working hard to create wealth you will want to take measures to protect it. This protection is a hedge against the unexpected. No one knows what the next moment brings, so be sure to cover yourself. You aren't wishing for bad things to find you, but it never hurts to minimize their harm if they do.

You have to remember that you cannot tell what will happen in the future. This means that no matter what you do, something unexpected can and will happen. For that reason, appreciate diversification.

> ## Rule #7: Don't put all your eggs in one basket.

An army that commits all of its soldiers to one location is only one mistake away from annihilation. No matter how well you plan, you cannot control every element of life. Someone told me "put all your eggs in one basket and then protect that basket with everything you have." This is simply foolish arrogance. The fact is you can't protect yourself against every potential calamity. A car crash, cancer, economic collapse, a new product that makes your obsolete - there are millions of things completely out of your control. The man who thinks he controls everything is a fool.

So the lesson here is simple, put your money to work in multiple areas. For me, this means a lot of my money is tied up in small businesses that I can influence, but that are in different markets and even different countries. I also allocate money to real estate, precious metals, and cash. If the real estate market in my hometown crashes, I will still have income from properties in other areas. I can't stop a tornado from destroying my rental property in Texas, but I can ensure my assets are distributed in multiple areas so that they are not all destroyed by the same storm.

Diversification into multiple types of assets will allow your army to grow regardless of the current economy or world politics. I have friends that are now struggling to rebuild their wealth because they didn't buy the right kind of insurance and instead bought into the fallacy that real estate is a risk free investment and were ultimately blindsided by the housing market crash. If they had only spent some time to diversify, they would not be in the position they are in today.

I routinely tell people to just look around them to see what would be best for their army. Look for items that have a historical relationship like the items below.

- Stock market down = gold up (Look at charts from late 2008-mid 2009)

- Oil down = travel/hospitality up

- Interest rates down = real estate development up

A Short Word on Insurance

In addition to diversifying your assets, you can also increase your protection by getting paid when something bad happens. You can pay a small amount of money now to ensure that you get a lot of money later if something bad happens. This is called insurance, and it is one of the greatest inventions of the modern world.

Rule #8: Buy insurance for your eggs, in case you drop the basket!

There are thousands of different types of insurance policies available, but don't feel overwhelmed. Make sure you cover the basics and expand coverage as you gain knowledge. To start, you should have some basic traditional insurance in place (home, health, auto, life). These will help you maintain a basic level of affluence if calamity strikes. I encourage you to do some research on insurance policies, run the numbers yourself (DO NOT take the advice of any insurance salesman without running the numbers yourself), and buy into policies that make sense for your situation.

AVOID FOOLISH LOANS

This is one of the hardest rules for the majority of people to follow. We live in a society that tells us that if we want something, then we can immediately have it. If we don't have the money on hand, we can get a loan or credit card to pay for it and then we pay interest to someone else instead of to our army. This is a foolish loan.

> *Rule #9: Only borrow money to buy assets*

I know I know, but Taylor how else am I going to get that dream house? Go back and read Chapter 2 now…

What if instead of saying "I have to get a loan in order to afford a house" we start to ask "what asset can I use to pay for that house?" When we use our assets to purchase our desires, we can truly experience freedom. A very basic example of this is using the dividends from your portfolio of stocks to pay for your country club membership.

Don't take foolish loans and don't make foolish loans. When you have money, you will be approached by people asking for loans. Some will be family, some will be friends, some will be strangers with really incredible plans for making a ton of money. My advice is this: if that person has not learned these lessons on wealth, they will not properly take care of your money. I lean on Luke 16:10 a lot for these scenarios, "he that is not faithful with a little, will not be faithful with a lot."

AVOID FOOLISH RISK

"Every fool must learn,' he growled, 'but why trust the knowledge of a brick maker about jewels? Would you go to the bread maker to inquire about the stars? No, by my tunic, you would go to the astrologer, if you had power to think. Your savings are gone, youth; you have jerked your wealth tree up by the roots. But plant another. Try again. And next time if you would have advice about jewels, go to the jewel merchant. If you would know the truth about sheep, go to the herdsman."

> ### Rule #10: Use your head, not your heart

I love this short paragraph from George S. Clason's book "The Richest Man in Babylon" because it so eloquently puts into words why so many people today still live without wealth, even though they save money. When it comes to creating your army of investments, you must, at all costs, avoid unnecessary and foolish risk. Just like we discussed in Chapter 2, if you take the advice of a random friend about an investment that he knows nothing about then you might as well count that money as gone and start again.

When researching potential assets to add to your army, seek out and meet with people who have experience in those areas. With the power of the internet (Facebook, Linkedin, Twitter, etc) at your disposal, it is easier now than ever to interview and meet people, even if they do not live near you. I am blessed to call many powerful and influential people friends because I was curious enough to pick up the phone or shoot off an email asking them for advice.

So my last lesson is this: surround yourself with smart, honest people who will help you achieve freedom through wealth. If you hang out at the donut shop, don't be surprised if you gain weight. If you hang out with successful people, your odds of being successful increase exponentially.

With that said, if you are interested in success and prosperity (and are honest and ethical), I would love to meet you. My contact information is available online at www.TaylorKovar.com

God bless you on your financial journey!

SCRIPTURES OF ENCOURAGEMENT

Ecclesiastes 8:7

Since no man knows the future, who can tell him what is to come?

1 Timothy 5:8

But if anyone does not provide for his relatives, and especially for members of his household, he has denied the faith and is worse than an unbeliever.

Acts 20:35

In all things I have shown you that by working hard in this way we must help the weak and remember the words of the Lord Jesus, how he himself said, 'It is more blessed to give than to receive.'

Ephesians 4:28

Let the thief no longer steal, but rather let him labor, doing honest work with his own hands, so that he may have something to share with anyone in need.

REFERENCES, SOURCES, AND ACKNOWLEDGEMENTS

This book draws on the wisdom, knowledge, and instruction of many people and sources. Here are just a few of the ones that had the biggest influence:

The Christian Bible, especially the books of Proverbs and Ecclesiastes

The Richest Man in Babylon by George S. Clason

Rich Dad, Poor Dad by Robert Kiyosaki

The Autobiography of Benjamin Franklin

The Millionaire Next Door by Thomas J Stanley